Editorial consultant: Mitch Cronick

CA58816

CONTENTS

Words in **bold** are explained in the glossary.

Trucks

Trucks have a **cab** where the driver sits.

Trucks have wheels with thick tyres.

Sometimes truck drivers sleep in the cab at night.

Engines

Trucks have an engine.

The engine makes the truck go.

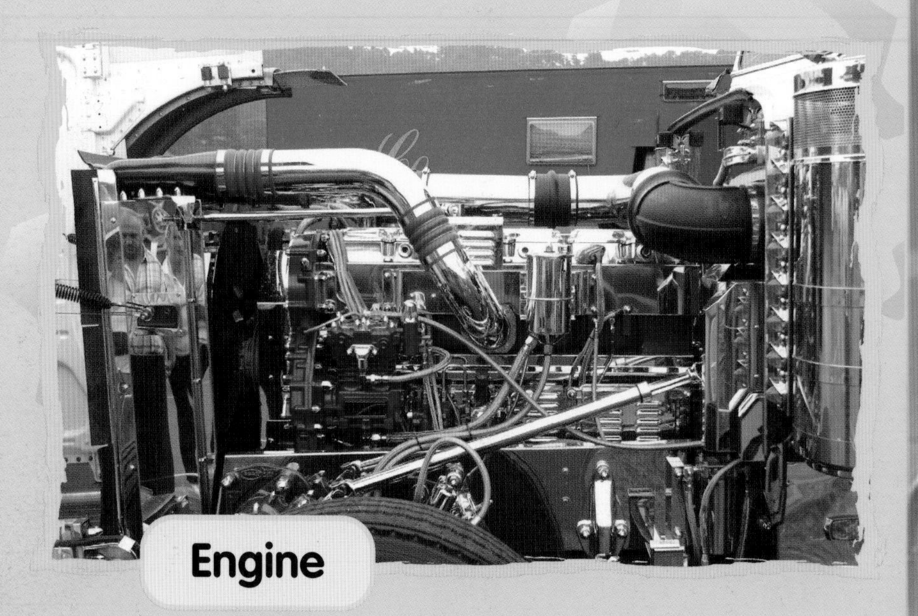

Engine

Trucks have an exhaust.

The exhaust takes gas away from the engine.

Exhaust
CATERPILLAR

Cab-over trucks

The cab is over the engine on some trucks.

These are called cab-over trucks.

On other trucks the cab is behind the engine.

Trucks with two parts

Some trucks have two parts.

The front part is the tractor.

The back part is the trailer.

The tractor has a cab, an engine and wheels.

Car transporters

These trucks carry cars.

At the front is the tractor.

The cars are on the trailer at the back.

FL10
INTERCOOLER

Road trains

Road trains go across **Australia**.

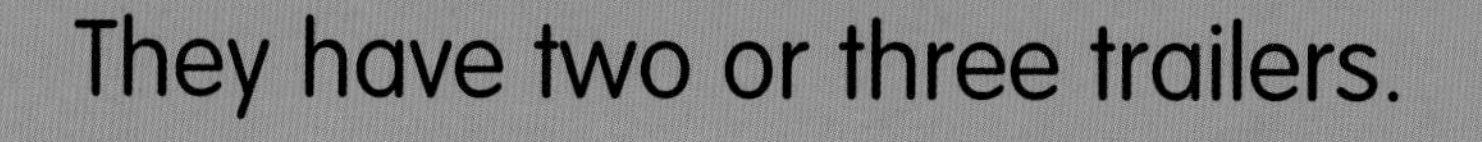

They have two or three trailers.

They have bars
that stop kangaroos
hitting the truck.

Bars

Trailers

Refuse trucks

Refuse trucks take away rubbish.

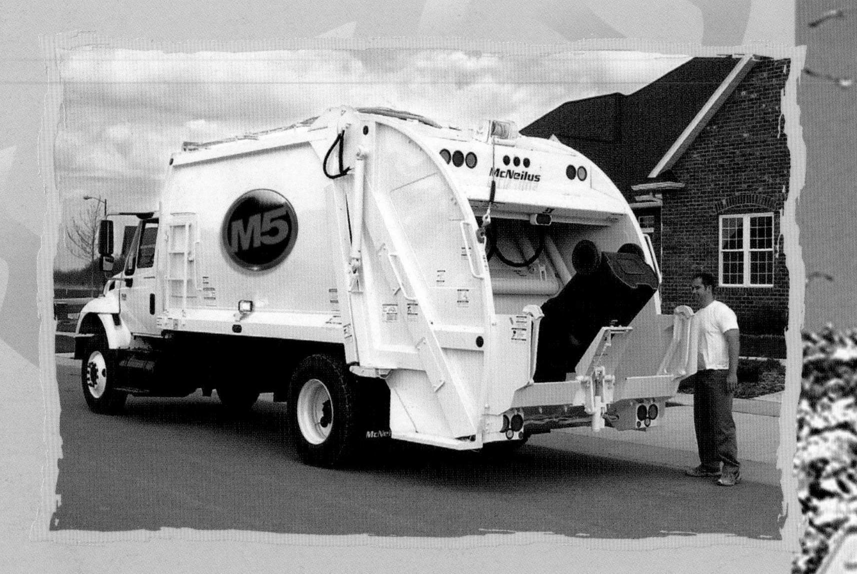

The rubbish goes into the back of the truck.

Then the rubbish is crushed.

The crushed rubbish is taken to a **tip**.

Tankers

Tankers are trucks with **tanks** at the back.

They carry milk or oil or petrol or gas.

Tank of petrol

This road train has
two tanks.

Mixer trucks

Mixer trucks carry water, cement, sand and gravel to make concrete.

They have big drums that turn around and mix the **concrete**.

The concrete comes
down a chute.
Chute
Concrete
Since 1946
61

Glossary

Australia

A very large country where kangaroos live.

cab

The part of a truck where the driver sits.

concrete
A mix of cement, water, sand and gravel used to build roads and buildings.

tank
A large container used to store liquids or gases.

tip
An large outdoor place where rubbish is left.

Index

First published in Great Britain in 2008 by **ticktock Media Ltd**.,
Unit 2, Orchard Business Centre, North Farm Road, Tunbridge Wells, Kent TN2 3XF
ISBN 978 1 84696 758 0 pbk
Printed in China

A CIP catalogue record for this book is available from the British Library.

We would like to thank: Penny Worms, Shirley Bickler, Suzanne Baker and the National Literacy Trust.

Picture credits (t=top, b=bottom, c=centre, l-left, r=right, OFC= outside front cover)
Alvey & Towers: 5. Peterbilt: 7, 9, 10-11, 22b. Shutterstock: 14-15. Superstock: 4, 6, 19, 21, 22t. ticktock photography: 1, 8, 9, 12, 13, 16-17, 18b, 20, 22m, 23t.

Every effort has been made to trace the copyright holders, and we apologise in advance for any unintentional omissions. We would be pleased to insert the appropriate acknowledgements in any subsequent edition of this publication.